# Data Analytics

*An Introduction and Explanation into Predictive Analysis (How to Integrate Analytics into Your Business).*

© Copyright 2017 Connection Books Club- All Rights Reserved.

This document is presented with the desire to provide reliable, quality information about the topic in question and the facts discussed within. This Book is sold under the assumption that neither the publisher or the author should be asked to provide the services discussed within. If any discussion, professional or legal, is otherwise required a proper professional should be consulted.

The reproduction, duplication or transmission of any of the included information is considered illegal whether done in print or electronically. Creating a recorded copy or a secondary copy of this work is also prohibited unless the action of doing so is first cleared through the Publisher and condoned in writing. All rights reserved.

Any information contained in the following pages is considered accurate and truthful and that any liability through inattention or by any use or misuse of the topics discussed within falls solely on the reader. There are no cases in which the Publisher of this work can be held responsible or be asked to provide reparations for any loss of monetary gain or other damages which may be caused by following the presented information in any way shape or form.

The following information is presented purely for informative purposes and is therefore considered universal. The information presented within is done so without a contract or any other type of assurance as to its quality or validity.

Any trademarks which are used are done so without consent and any use of the same does not imply consent or permission was gained from the owner. Any trademarks or brands found within are purely used for clarification purposes and no owners are in anyway affiliated with this work.

# Table of Contents

Introduction ........................................................................... 1
Understanding Data Analytics ................................................ 4
Understanding Predictive Analysis........................................ 12
Applications Of Predicative Analysis ................................... 17
Data Gathering ..................................................................... 25
Data Mining ......................................................................... 32
Data Prediction Techniques-Regression .............................. 39
Data Prediction Techniques-Machine Learning.................. 45
Utilizing Discrete Choice Models ........................................ 52
Data Management Mistakes To Avoid................................ 59
Starter Software To Collect Data ......................................... 66
Conclusion Wrap Up: Data Analysis Overview................. 76

# Introduction

Congratulations on downloading *Data Analytics: An Introduction and Explanation into Predictive Analysis (How to Integrate Analytics into Your Business)*, and thank you for doing so. Understanding the data that your business is already generating every day is a key to success in the Big Data World that you are competing in, and purchasing this book is a great step in the right direction.

It is only the first step, however, which is why the following chapters will discuss everything you need to know about data analytics in general and predictive analysis specifically. This means there are detailed chapters on data gathering, data mining, regression techniques, machine learning techniques, discrete choice models and more. You will also find an in-depth look at many of the most common mistakes that companies make when it comes to data management and how to avoid them. Finally, things will wrap up with a detailed discussion of the best open source programs that can have you analyzing data this very night.

There are plenty of books on this subject on the market – thanks again for choosing this one! Every effort was made to ensure it is full of as much useful information as possible, please enjoy!

Thank you for your purchase of this eBook! I hope you enjoy reading this eBook as much as I enjoyed writing it. As part of your purchase, I invite you to join my email subscribers. This FREE subscription lets you receive a newsletter, highlighting the great new books available from Connection Books Club and other exclusive business and self development information. Subscribing is easy, and members receive great deals and fantastic eBooks at a discount! All you need to do is click this link to enter your email:

http://www.connectionbooksclub.com/bonus/

In addition to this great opportunity to subscribe to incredible discounts and our newsletter, as a welcome gift, you'll receive a FREE eBook download! Learn how to secure your financial future with the informative eBook, *Money Management: Learn How to Organize Your Financial Life and Invest in Your Future*. It's yours for FREE once you've enrolled!

http://www.connectionbooksclub.com/bonus/

Welcome to the club, and we hope you enjoy your purchase as well as our FREE welcome gift!

**Have you ever wished that you were better with money?**

**Do you ever find yourself being overwhelmed by the state of your personal finances?**

**Would you like to become more financially responsible?**

Now you can, with **5 Reasons to Invest in Money Management: Learn How to Organize Your Financial Life and Invest in Your Future**, a short self-help book that is packed with information on how to make the most of your financial situation.

If you want to be able to lower your interest rates, learn up to date money management strategies and turn your financial situation into one of prosperity and stability, then you'll find the answers inside, with solid advice that includes:

- ➤ **Strategies which are designed for the average person**
- ➤ **Your options for retirement**
- ➤ **Hacks for navigating the grocery store's subtle spending traps**
- ➤ **Ways to pay less than you owe on credit cards and other outstanding debts**
- ➤ **Finding freedom with financial stability**

Suitable for complete novices, **5 Reasons to Invest in Money Management** is a book that will transform the way you look at and deal with your finances.

Download a free copy and start investing in your future today! http://www.connectionbooksclub.com/bonus/

Prosperity is waiting for **YOU!**

# Understanding Data Analytics

One of the most common buzzwords floating around online today is data analysis, and while you may have heard of it, figuring out exactly what it means might be more difficult than you might expect. The reason for this is that there are several different definitions for the phrase depending on who you ask. While it can mean more specific things in context, in general, a definition that you can work with is that it is the process by which data is modeled, transformed, cleaned and inspected by businesses, with the ultimate goal being its use in the decision-making process.

As such, this makes a data analyst the person whose job it is to find the best answers to the questions that businesses come up with. They take the lines and lines of data that they find and paint a clear picture of just what it means so that those without the skills to see the pictures in the data still have a firm grasp on what is going on in the market or even with their very own businesses. The data that is analyzed varies radically based on the business that is looking and what it is they are looking for, so much so that it is currently created at a rate of more than 2 quintillion bytes each day worldwide.

This dramatic influx in what is available has not gone unnoticed, and businesses everywhere are getting in on the mega trend of collecting data and analyzing it as quickly and effectively as possible. When it comes to finding the truth at the heart of the data, the deeper and more accurate of an insight you can find, the more easily you will be able to discover the hidden trends that are hiding and use them as effectively, and profit from them. This is primarily done through the use of statistical analysis, including both the predictive types of modeling that will be discussed in the following chapters, as well as explanatory modeling which is a complex enough topic on its own to warrant discussion at another time.

It is especially useful as it can be used equally effectively by both automated and human-driven decisions. What it all boils down to, is that traditional business intelligence can often be used to determine what a specific problem is, how often it occurs, where an issue is located and, even, how it can be fixed, but good analytics can determine the source of the problem in the first place as well as what is likely going to happen if the current trends continue.

## Evolving Usage

Analytics have been in near constant use since a variety of time-management exercises were first instituted by a man named Frederick Winslow Taylor in the 1800s. Taylor was an engineer who was fascinated with the idea of industrial efficiency and what it could mean for businesses of all shapes and sizes. While working as a foreman at the Midvale Steel Works, Taylor expected his team to work as hard as they could without causing themselves injury or undue stress. To determine how to do this, he started by analyzing the productivity of the men in his charge as well as the machines that they were working with. Taylor went on to use his insights to shape the field of scientific management, of which data analytics is a part.

While used in a limited fashion, most notably by Henry Ford to dictate the pacing of his assembly lines, the value of analytics was not truly grasped by a wider group of individuals until computers started to be able to utilize it as a way of implementing decision support systems in the 1960s. With the power of the burgeoning computer sciences behind then, analytics have since evolved into numerous different applications, software tools, and hardware, and include things as varied as data warehouses and enterprise resource-planning systems.

What this means for businesses today is that every business has some data that is crucial for their operations and extended success and existence. Knowing what this data is and utilizing it effectively are two different things, however, which is where data analytics comes in.

## Putting Data Analytics to Work

When it comes to analyzing the data that you are presented with, the first thing you are going to want to do is determine if the data that you are preparing to analyze is going to add real value to your business as a whole or if the costs are not going to be worth the time and effort needed to gather them properly. For example, going through all of your sales data in order to determine the most popular product or service you provide, as well as which is the most profitable, will provide you with clear pillars of your business to focus on in order to ensure you are as successful as possible in both the short and the long term.

This activity is a productive use of time because it can help you to accurately predict what the future of your business could look like under certain market conditions. Once those conditions have been properly pinpointed, they can then be used as a direction for the business to move in the short term. By default, the above example also serves another, potentially more important, purpose; it shows you what products or services that you are offering that absolutely no one is interested in taking you up on. As such, you would then be able to more accurately determine if there might not be a better use of your company's resources than the underperforming products. Either way, a byproduct of the process is a reduction of waste as well as an increase in sales revenue.

*Targeting the right data:* To understand the right type of data you are going to want to target, it is important to understand that it primarily comes in two forms, those that are structured, such as traditional databases, and those that are unstructured, things like social media networks or phone applications that rely on data sent over the internet. With so much data to keep track of, you may find it helpful to set up an automated method of collection when it comes to your daily transaction output to ensure that any future analysis is done with data that is as straight from the source as possible.

This, in turn, means that you will need to determine the right database structure for the data that you are going to be retrieving and the way you are going to want to access it later if you hope to see the best results. Choosing the right type of database for your business is an important choice and one which is discussed several times in the following pages.

However, if you instead plan on determining the current public sentiment that your customers have towards your business, then you are going to want to analyze online applications and social media profiles, the two places that people are prone to leaving feedback in the ever-connected world of the twenty-first century. Ways for doing so are discussed in the following chapters, and are also always being created, so if you are interested in keeping on top of this field you will always need to be on the lookout for new trends.

*Determine the best type of analysis:* After you have found the data that you are looking for, the next thing you are going to want to do is determine the most effective type of analysis that you can use to get at the heart of the data. There are numerous different tools as well as platforms for analysis on the market and determining the right one for you is going to mean looking at the ways your business operates and coming up with the right solution based on what you find. The details on how to choose the right tools for the job, as well as what to do once you have them are described in later chapters.

## Big Data Defined

Due to the often fluid nature of the data analytics field, it is perfectly natural for certain myths to crop up surrounding its specifics. The biggest and most outlandish of these is that data analytics are only useful for large corporations or businesses with more data coming in than they can analyze. In reality, however, it is important to understand that analyzing the data that you do have available is an excellent choice regardless of the size of your business or the amount of data you can access.

Focusing on the size of your business or the limited nature of the data that you can find means focusing on the wrong issues. Instead, it is important that you look to determine if the data that you do have access to can actually be useful in a real and meaningful way. If you have access to data that you think can be useful then, it is important to seek out ways to utilize it, to your benefit.

These myths are often further segmented once concepts like Big Data enter the conversation. While the term 'big data' is new, however, the data that it represents has been around for nearly 20 years if not longer. Big Data can essentially be thought of as all of the data that is owned by a company and also what the company does with that data, which can be scrutinized for relative trends. The problem with Big Data, however, is in the name, which means that there is just so much of it to go through that it can be difficult to see the big picture without organizing it.

## Big Data Pros and Cons

While it might be difficult to tap into, interpreting Big Data is a vital step to succeeding in the modern marketplace where major companies are literally constantly combing their data for even a tangential increase in dominance against their competition. That doesn't mean that it is the right choice in every situation, however, consider the following pros and cons and you should come away with a better idea of just whether or not monitoring it is the right choice for you and your business.

*Pros:* First and foremost, combing through Big Data can lead to competitive advantages based on results generated from the software of your choice that can lead to a clear highlighting of asymmetrical elements related to your marketing or production plans. An example of what makes this type of information so useful can be seen in the hockey sport as demonstrated by the 2009 Vancouver Canucks. Now, prior to 2009, the Canucks and every other hockey team, matched the power of the opposing team's players head for head, which meant that the stars from both teams always faced off against one another. A data analyst for the

Canucks looked into this fact and realized something surprising; there was a better way of playing. Thanks to the wide variety of data available, the Canucks were able to shake things up and see an increased win rate that season because of it.

Additionally, Big Data can be useful if you are reporting to a board of directors. Once it is demonstrated that it can clearly show the right moves for a given business at a given point and time, it becomes a big step forward for many data analysts who have traditionally been ignored at the board level for other, more popular, strategies. This mindset has been changing over the past decade, and now, having Big Data behind your plan is a big point in your favor.

Finally, access to Big Data can regularly lead to major new startups or innovative products in either existing or entirely new fields. Businesses that are built on innovation need only harness the power of Big Data to be able to figure out the market's demands and desires for new products.

*Cons:* On the other hand, there is no denying that Big Data is also the latest in a long line of trending business-centric buzzwords such as Web 2.0. In fact, much of what is currently under the banner of Big Data was, until 2013, most commonly referred to business intelligence. As such, it is important to keep in mind that while it may be useful, Big Data is hardly the be-all-end-all that some people are eager to make it out to be. As such, if, after trying to make things work for you and your business, Big Data doesn't seem to be the right choice for you, you don't need to feel bad about looking in other directions instead.

Additionally, when it comes to looking for Big Data, you are going to be sure that you have a large amount of relevant data that can be transmitted rapidly, and that comes in multiple types. Typically, these types include primarily, demographic preferences, past purchases, SMS statistics, engagement email statistics and overall site statistics. However, if the data you are looking at is all either structured or unstructured, then you don't necessarily need Big Data methodologies so much as you need a way to parse a few small sets of data. Ensure the data you are using is interconnected for the best results.

Finally, when using Big Data, it can be easy to use too much data in an effort to create a perfect formula for every situation. This can't really be done, unfortunately, which is why Big Data can accurately predict the past with 100 percent accuracy while still not getting the future just right. If you are hoping to use Big Data to tell you the future, then you are going to want things to be exactly as they were in the past which is never a sure thing as there are too many variables to account for. As such, Big Data can show you trends, it can't predict the future.

# Understanding Predictive Analysis

Predictive analytics is all about insight into the future without having to rely on hindsight after the fact. If analytics can be thought of as the communication and discovery of relevant patterns in various types of customers, channels, products and corporate data, then it can further be broken down in several different ways. If you are interested in figuring out when and where a specific event took place, then you are interested in descriptive analytics. If you are interested in getting to the bottom of why an event took place, then you can use either prescriptive analytics or diagnostic analytics, and if you are interested in learning what is likely to happen in the future then you are interested in predictive analytics.

Predictive analytics is successful based on its reliance on a handful of crucial techniques that create information that is worth acting upon out of a wide variety of data that often appears random at first. These are predictive searches or machine learning that is supervised, transaction profiling, decision analysis and optimization and predictive modeling. Each of these is integral to the predictive model and will be outlined in detail below.

*Predictive Modeling:* Mathematically, predictive modeling represents the direct, if often hidden relationships concealed in various types of data. These relationships are then typically used as a means of predicting, classifying or forecasting future events. Predictive models are useful when it comes time to analyze historical or current data as it relates to individuals, because they can be used to generate metrics related to various scores that have been assigned. These scores, in turn, can be used to rank different products, services or individuals based on the predicted likelihood of future performance.

Additionally, it is important to note that predictive models are also useful when it comes to detecting the likelihood of fraud or failure occurring. This is why they are often used in transaction systems that are considered critical to the successful long-term functioning of the business where they can help keep decisions on track in practically real time. This process, in turn, is borne on the backs of several different relevant methodologies, briefly described below. They include:

- Mathematical algorithms for programing, including applications of both nonlinear and linear mathematics. In these instances, the objective is always going to remain optimized to a specific set of constraints.

- Neural systems can also be used to find vast and complicated patterns in very large data sets that can then be utilized to successfully predict when a certain variable is likely to express a certain set of behaviors or characteristics. Also referred to as Deep Learning Systems, these are the types of systems that are used for speech or picture recognition systems.

- Alternatively, statistical analysis techniques can also be used to detect patterns in larger-than-average data sets.

Regardless of the specifics of how they go about doing it, predictive models are generally going to be the most useful when they are used to summarize large data sets.

*Optimization of Decision Analysis:* Decision analysis is the practice of analyzing, modeling and optimizing decisions that organizations, groups or individuals make. Additional applications include things like determining operating costs, finding otherwise easily missed sales opportunities, finding the best performance indicators and optimizing how supply chains are managed. Predictive models are useful when it comes to looking more closely at various aspects of past behavior to predict future behavior; decision analysis, on the other hand, is useful when it comes to looking at different angles of a particular choice in an effort to determine what the best course of action moving forward might entail.

The focus here is on understanding the challenges that your business faces and the various options you have at any given moment when it comes to finding the best solution. The best decision analysis plans tend to focus on mathematically mapping out the decision structure and all its possible outcomes. In order for this type of approach to work, it requires a method for continuously learning as well as constant extrapolation of the current strategy and how it would rate against scenarios that have not yet been encountered.

*Transaction Profiling:* Transaction profiling can be useful when it comes to minimizing the complexity of the current data regarding transactions, for the purpose of modeling, in order to ensure the information that is extracted is as useful as possible. This is especially relevant when it comes to monitoring data that changes over time such as credit card transactions which can otherwise be quite difficult to use in a standard predictive model. This is caused due to a combination of elements, the first of which is that each individual transaction holds relatively little useful information, especially when it comes to divining the habits of the person who made the purchase in the first place. Added to this is the fact that the transaction patterns of an individual can vary drastically over a short period of time for few obvious reasons.

To overcome these handicaps, it is important to use the right techniques in order to turn the raw data into something that can reveal additional useful information. This makes the data more worthwhile when it comes to predictive models, and thus, overall. This technology is at its best when it is utilizing data from many different types of transactions to create profiles related to different patterns of transactions. These profiles can then be used to effectively and efficiently make assessments that are more likely to be on the money when it comes to things like credit risk or fraud risk in other, related, streams.

*Predictive Search:* Also known as deep learning, predictive search via machine learning that is supervised is considered by many to be the future of engaging the consumer as successfully as possible. In this case, the machines are a type of software that can essentially teach itself to recognize a range of spoken dialogue, text, objects and more. Additionally, each year sees greater and greater advancement when it comes to the way that humans interface with the software and interact with it on the most basic level. The most common examples of this these days are Siri in Apple products and Cortana in Windows 10.

In this instance, the signals in the data are uncovered based on what the software has been told to look for and how it is supposed to respond when it comes across a certain pattern. While this technology is still relatively nascent, it will soon be used in a variety of instances outside of its prevalence in social media networks. Easy examples include retailers being able to automatically send out coupons to consumers who suddenly drop off from a previously higher rate of consumption of products or services or automatic messages that are sent once a potential client reaches a certain radius from a related product.

*What to Do with the Data:* Regardless of where your data comes from, the most important thing is always going to be acting on it in the most productive way possible. Remember, having the insight into a given course of action isn't worth anything if you don't know how to act on it, and the best state of action is one that is automatic when the insight occurs. This can be easier said than done, however, as it requires the right mix of closed-loop decision analytics, mindset, skill set, data set and tool set.

Your goal should be, first and foremost, to ensure that you have the foundation in place to handle the volume of the data that you are going to want to compile. Aside from that, you are going to want ensure you can ask the right questions of your data so that you can be sure it will ultimately be successful. Data discovery is a great way of getting to data that otherwise appears locked.

*Predictive Analytic Providers:* Generating the Big Data that predictive analytics requires is done both in regulated and unregulated ways. This type of information is collected in a regulated fashion by those working in the wealth or health markets and in an unregulated fashion in the publishing, media and retail markets. Furthermore, analytic information can be gained from the marketing services sector from vendors who are competing with more traditional advertising agencies as well as analytic and information technology companies. Additionally, there will be vendors in the customer management, fraud solutions and originations market that offer up a range of relevant data as well.

# Applications of Predicative Analysis

While predictive analysis can be applied to virtually any type of business or function in business, once the unique aspect of that business are taken into account, some more naturally analytical businesses are outlined below.

*Customer Relationship Management:* When it comes to managing customer relationships in an analytical fashion, many business owners find this to be a natural fit for predictive analysis. Predictive analysis methods are then used to determine the relevance of various types of consumer data when it comes to determining what is considered an all-around holistic view of the customer in question, regardless of where their information may have been obtained from. Additionally, this type of analysis will be used when it comes to determining effective sales campaigns, marketing advertisements and what services customers should be provided with.

Using predictive analysis in this way can be especially effective if a company has a broad customer base and is interested in ensuring that no segment of it is accidentally going to be left behind. Specifically, this is done by analyzing what products are currently in the highest demand and what customers' buying habits are likely going to be for both the short and the long term. Finally, when used properly, it will be helpful in spotting, and preventing issues that might appear in the future were they to be left untreated. These are the types of issues that can often grow slowly and fester within a business if left untreated, costing them customers all the while.

This kind of analysis can be useful throughout the life of the average customer relationship, first during the acquisition phase, then again during the relationship growth phase, once more during the retention phase and then a final time if they end up in a win-back phase. Additionally, many of the applications outlined below can also be used to manage the relationship with your customers successfully.

*Child protection:* In the past decade, the popularity of predictive analytics for use in child welfare situations has increased dramatically. This is an excellent example of where machine thinking can get to the heart of a complicated matter which goes unreported by living, breathing individuals, who can come up with perfectly valid reasons why the evidence doesn't seem to add up in the way that it first appears. This trend appears to be so effective that it has dramatically decreased the overall amount of abuse, as well as cut down all deaths related to abuse in the area it was tested in.

*Health care support systems to support clinical decisions:* Predictive analysis in health care is primarily used as a tool to determine if a given patient is at an increased risk of developing numerous conditions including lifetime illnesses such as heart disease, asthma, and diabetes. Furthermore, there are numerous point-of-care clinical decision support systems for numerous types of emergencies that are literally life or death. These systems provide patients, staff, and clinicians with access to information on a specific person that is filtered or presented only when the need arises to make the transfer of information between individuals a less convoluted and all-round smoother process. It is known to encompass a wide variety of interventions and tools, including things like clinical workflow tools diagnostic support, documentation templates, patient data, order sets, clinical guidelines, reminders and computerized alerts all designed with the aim of making any hospital visit safer for the patient and easier to handle for the staff.

As recently as the summer of 2016, major breakthroughs are being made in this field, specifically when it comes to the study of various neurodegenerative issues, including Parkinson's disease. Using a specifically designed support system platform, as well as lots of demographic, clinical genetic, and multi-source imaging data, the researchers who developed the platform were able to successfully determine the rate of progress of the disease with a greater degree of accuracy than ever before. Even better, the underlying facts of the study are promising when it comes to adapting the technology to work for a variety of other diseases including Amyotrophic Lateral Sclerosis, Huntington's Disease and even Alzheimer's Disease.

*Collection Analytics:* Regardless of the business you are in, if you work with customers on credit, then you are going to find yourself going up against customers who refuse to pay their bills on time, if at all. Luckily, predictive analytics can be useful in this field as well, both as a way of determining if a specific customer is going to be a risk as far as their credit history is indication of reliability; but also when it comes to determining if it is going to be worth it to try and actually get the money back. While on paper it seems as though it would make sense to go after everyone who owes your company money, in reality that is simply not the case, and some funds will simply be too difficult or downright impossible to recover under normal circumstances.

As such, the use of predictive analytics is effective when it comes to analyzing the overall best-case scenario when it comes to the allocation of resources to maximize debt consolidation activities. This, in turn, results in a dramatic increase in the recovery rate of the assets that are actively pursued, so much so that it actually recoups a significantly higher amount than if everyone was pursued equally.

*Cross sell:* When corporate organizations collect vast amounts of data, one of the most important types of relationships that they are looking for is the relationships that indicate if the purchase of one item increases the likelihood that the same person would then purchase another item. Using predictive analytics for this type of analysis will allow you to analyze things like usage metrics and spending habits, which will, in turn, lead to cross sales that are followed through to completion at a much higher rate than what might otherwise be the case. This then directly correlates to not only a higher overall rate of individual customer profitability but also stronger relationships with individual customers overall.

*Customer retention:* Thanks to the internet, hundreds of your competitors can be found with the click of a couple of buttons, which means that if your customer retention isn't at the highest rate it can be at, then you are on the razor's edge of losing out on potential profit. Luckily, predictive analysis, in this case, can be used to minimize the attrition of existing customers by making it easier for you to reward customer loyalty, improve overall customer satisfaction and maintain customer focus on desired brands. While each one of these options might only raise your retention rates individually by a small amount, sometimes a small amount is all it really takes. In fact, studies show that a 5 percent increase in overall customer retention rates is good for anywhere from a 25 percent increase in profits to as much as a 100 percent increase in profits.

Predictive analysis is so effective in this instance because it lets you react to declining consumer interest, not after they have already entered the termination phase where they are already severing their ties with your brand, but instead earlier in the process where the chance of success is going to work out to be much better. In fact, studies show that trying to change a customer's mind once it has already been made up and they have initiated the termination phase is practically impossible. However, if you catch them earlier, then the odds default into them sticking with the established relationship rather than going through the work of finding someplace new.

By regularly examining each customer's purchase records, you can determine usage patterns and overall engagement rates. Understanding what phase customers are currently at will make it easier to determine when dips in the numbers actually do start to occur. When the numbers begin to drop noticeably, the best course of action is often going to be a lucrative offer which has been noted to change a flagging customer's mind about 50 percent of the time. In the face of a slow rate of attrition over time, the sweeping grand gesture often won't do the trick, however, which is why it is important to utilize predictive analytics to change the pattern before it reaches critical levels.

*Direct Marketing:* When it comes to marketing the products you are selling; you have several different challenges that you are going to need to overcome, including keeping up with customer interest and your competitors' products. While predictive analytics will make both of these things easier, it will also help you to determine the most effective option when it comes to identifying potentially profitable prospects, along with the most useful version of various products, communication channels, marking materials and timing that have the biggest impact on your target customer base. Predictive analysis shines in this instance because of its ability to lower your overall marketing cost per action.

*Fraud detection:* When it comes to loss leaders in certain sectors, fraud is definitely going to be near the top of the list. Fraud comes in many forms from downright fraudulent transactions to inaccurate applications to outright identity theft or false claims; but regardless of type, it all has the potential to cost your business money if you don't have the predictive analytic measures in place to ensure that you don't get swindled along with everyone else. Additionally, predictive modeling can be a useful way of identifying individual customers who use your products or services who might be a ripe target for fraud in the future, either as the perpetrator or the victim. Predictive analytics are so helpful when it comes to fraud detection that they are routinely used as a preventative measure by the IRS. Furthermore, advances are being made in the realm of online fraud prevention using predictive analytics as a guidepost.

*Product level prediction:* Predictive analytics is useful, not just when it comes to analyzing individuals, but also when it comes to analyzing the economy as a whole or various industries, firms, portfolios or even individual products. A good example of this occurs every time a retailer decides that they want to know what their demand is likely to be prior to reordering stock, or when the Federal Reserve needs to predict what unemployment is likely going to look like next year. These problems and others like them can all be addressed using what are known as predictive analytic series techniques (discussed in Chapter 4). Additionally, these answers can also be found through a vigorous application of machine-based learning approaches which can then utilize time-series data as a variation of traditional vector space, before then utilizing relevant learning algorithms in an effort to divine patterns and predict likelihoods relating to the future.

*Defining levels of risk:* When it comes to techniques that work to utilize risk management as effectively as possible, the end result is always going to be a prediction of the future. The information that predictive analysis provides can easily be useful outside of the individual project that is being worked on if the effort is taken to extend the data to the market as a whole over both the short and the long term.

*Underwriting:* Businesses of various types can often find themselves in need of a way to mitigate the risk that the business in question leaves them exposed to. This, in turn, leaves them in need of a way to determine how to pass those costs along to customers who might by their very nature prove to be more of a risk than the average customer. Through the use of predictive analytics, businesses can streamline the process of looking into the details of every customer by applying a variety of different parameters that, in turn, relate to different levels of assumed risk. This type of predictive analytics can readily be seen in the form of credit scores, which have dramatically reduced the work that is required by lenders when it comes to approving a wide variety of loans, often cutting days, if not weeks, off of the time that it takes to make these types of decisions.

Enjoying your eBook so far? Take a moment to subscribe to our FREE newsletter for incredible discounts, books giveaways, and VIP offers!

- http://www.connectionbooksclub.com/bonus/

All we need is your email, and you'll be set up to receive more of the eBooks you can't wait to read.

# Data Gathering

Now that you have a clearer idea of what predictive analytics is, and how it can be useful to your business, the next thing you are going to need to learn is all about the data you will soon be sifting through. This chapter will cover where you will be keeping all of your business data, as well as how you are going to gather it and mine it for the most useful information possible.

## Data Warehouse

A data warehouse is a special type of warehouse that is specifically designed to make it easier for you to interact with the data that you store on it. Essentially, it is designed from the ground up with the intent of making it as easy as possible to analyze and query data, as opposed to processing transactions, which means it can contain a variety of data aside from a simple list of transactions.

Additionally, data warehouses separate workload into two parts, the analysis portion and the transaction portion, which in turn helps in several different ways. These include making it easier to maintain records as well improving the rate at which data can be analyzed and thus improving stakeholder understanding of the state of the business as a whole. A data warehouse is typically capable of storing years and years of relevant data at a time; it is also becoming increasingly common for these databases to contain a program that automatically transforms it as the database requires.

While their specifics are likely to vary, all data warehouse have a few core characteristics in common. First and foremost, the database that you decide on should be specifically designed for the subject you plan on tracking in it. You will want to have various types of warehouses: one that focuses on sales, another that focuses on customers, etc. Next, you are going to want to ensure that your warehouse has the ability to ensure that all of the different types of content that you are going to be using can be placed into a universal format. Taking note of this ability has the potential to save you literally hundreds of hours in the long run and is extremely recommended.

Additionally, you are going to want to ensure that your database has a history of being nonvolatile, even when changing between versions or machines. It is crucial to the long-term success of your predictive analysis that your system essentials remain as nonvolatile as possible at all times. Finally, you are going to want to ensure that your data warehouse is designed in such a way that its focus can change over time, which is referred to in predictive analytics as a time variant.

Outside of these core characteristics, you are going to want to ensure that your data is structured as simply as possible to ensure the best access speeds possible are always available. Each query that you make to the database should also return as much data as possible, sometimes even thousands and thousands of rows. What's more, these queries should have the ability to be ad hoc as well as predefined and they should look through multiple sources as well as multiple transformations in order to arrive at the results that you ultimately see.

## Data Gathering

When it comes time to actually start collecting your data, there are numerous different ways you can go about doing so, many of which are outlined below, including what their purpose might be, what advantages they bring to the table and the various challenges you might face when implementing them.

### Checklists, Surveys, and Questionnaires

*Purpose:* Surveys, questionnaires, and checklists all serve similar purposes in that they are great ways of getting lots of information from your customers in a short period of time. They also work great with new customers who have no previous relationship with your business as they are typically considered both non-invasive and non-threatening.

*Advantages:* These types of information gathering techniques can be utilized extremely cheaply and analyzed without having to resort to extremely complicated methods of analysis. They are also great for gathering a wide variety of data all at once, and samples of all three are readily available online to get you started in the right direction.

*Challenges:* Challenges in this instance include the fact that there are numerous reasons that the validity of the data can be questioned while also not getting the full story behind the data that is obtained.

### Interview

*Purpose:* An interview is at its most relevant when the business in question is interested in learning the full story behind individual customers' experiences and impressions.

*Advantages:* Interviews are particularly great at getting a wide range of information from a customer while also getting deeper and more detailed information on specific topics of interest. Additionally, this is a great way to develop a closer relationship with various customers as it can be varied to fit individual situations.

*Challenges:* The biggest challenge that interviews face is that they require a large investment in man hours in order to see any results. This means they are often quite expensive as well as time-consuming when applied on a larger scale. Additionally, they can be hard to compare to one another depending on how different the various customer interactions turn out to be, or the interviewer and customer relationship could bias the results.

*Documentation Review*

*Purpose:* The purpose of a documentation review is to gain an impression of how a specific program operates while at the same time not hindering the program from going about its business. The sort of documentation that is being reviewed is going to vary by business, but will typically include things like minutes, memos, finances, and applications.

*Advantages:* The biggest advantage of performing a documentation review is that it provides you with access to a comprehensive review of historical information without requiring a loss in productivity to do so. Additionally, this is going to be a review of information that exists, which means additional costs are not going to be incurred while the data is collected.

*Challenges:* The biggest challenge that you will likely face during a documentation review is likely going to be how many documents you come across that are incomplete in one way or another. This in turn can make gathering relevant data take longer than it should, especially if you don't have a laser-sharp focus on the type of data that you are looking for. Finally, if you undertake a documentation review, you can easily be left with gaps in your information as you are limited to the information that you already have on hand.

*Observation*

*Purpose:* If you are curious about how a program is going to actually work when it is in play in the real world then observation is the best way to get to the bottom of things. It is especially useful when it comes to learning about the different processes that are working together to create the outcome in question.

*Advantages:* The biggest advantage to the observation method of gathering data is that it is extremely easy to update the process if something new occurs unexpectedly. Additionally, it is useful for its ability to view the various operations that go into a specific program as they are occurring. Finally, it is cost-effective as it does not require the program to go offline and can be done by just one person.

*Challenges:* If observation is useful when it comes to determining the relative success of various operations in a program, the biggest challenge then is to properly interpret the various operations in the program in the right way. Depending on the business and program in question, this sort of categorical observation can become very complex, very quickly. Finally, it is important to keep in mind that sometimes it can be hard to know if the fact that the operations are being observed is enough to influence their outcome.

*Focus Groups*

*Purpose:* The purpose of a focus group is to get a large group of either customers or employees together, depending on the type of information being gathered, with the goal of going deep on a topic and exploring it thoroughly. As a means of gathering data, focus groups shine when it comes to gathering data related to marketing or the otherwise evaluation of the topic in question.

*Advantages:* The biggest advantage of using a focus group is how easy and reliable you can gather a consensus opinion. Additionally, it is often considered one of the more efficient ways to gather a broader range of data that is also more in-depth than many of the types of data gathering methods. Finally, it makes it easy to see what type of information floats to the top, as it were, and comes across as key in relation to the topic in question,

*Challenges:* The biggest challenge when it comes to utilizing focus groups is that it can be hard to find deeper patterns in the data as it can easily become disparate without the right facilitator to keep things on track. Depending on the skills that you and your team can bring to bear, this means that things can get expensive quickly as a good focus group facilitator, while worth it if you choose to go down this route, can be pricey. Finally, if you are looking to get a specific group of six or more individuals together at one time, then you are likely going to experience some difficulty doing so.

*Case Studies*

*Purpose:* The purpose of a case study is to really get to the bottom of a specific client's experience with a given program. This is done through a detailed exanimation and repeated comparison to various other cases that contain the same parameters.

*Advantages:* The biggest advantage of doing a case study is that you gain access to data that completely details a certain client's experience with a given program, as well as all of their input about the event and its ultimate result. This type of data is known to be particularly compelling when viewed by those outside the team when it comes to getting a broad handle on a given program.

*Challenges:* The biggest challenge when it comes to running a case study is the amount of time that is required in order to describe, organize and collect all the data that is required to make the case study meaningful and relevant. Additionally, if depth and breadth existed on a spectrum, then a case study is all depth and no breadth.

# Data Mining

Data mining is the name that has been given to the process of finding the relevant trends within Big Data and then analyzing it for the benefit of the additional perspective it brings, before going on to find additional relationships hidden within the data. Data mining as a whole can be split into two primary types: descriptive, which is described in this chapter; and predictive, which is discussed in the next chapter.

## Data Mining Basic Requirements

If you plan on mining data on a regular basis, then the first thing you will need to do is to ensure that your data warehouse is in order as previously discussed. Additionally, you are going to want to find data analysis tools that are easy enough to use and comprehend that you don't need someone whose entire purpose is to know how to use them. Finally, you are going to want to ensure that the information that you do generate is going to be compatible with numerous different systems.

When it comes to deciding what tools you are going to want to use, you may find it useful to determine how they are going to be used in a conventional decision-making process. The first step of the decision-making process is to develop a style of reporting that is standardized. Next, it will be important to take note of any instances that might be an exception to the rule you have created. These exceptions could be positive and lead to advantages, or they could be negative and give you an insight into potential problems. Once exceptions have been noted you will want to determine important causes before looking into alternatives and determining the overall of what it is that you have decided.

Standard reports are any results that you pull using database queries, and they can determine how a business is performing as well as shed light on several other important business factors. When exceptions occur, however, then you want to know that the details will be easy to retrieve when needed.

## Clean Up the Data

When used in reference to data, the term *cleaning* refers to the action of eliminating data points that are invalid from a given set of data so that the remaining data can be utilized as effectively as possible. Invalid points of data can either be those that are only partially available, are corrupted, or do not factor into the hypothesis that is being used to analyze the data at this point. It is difficult to remove the cleaning step from the realm of human judgment as the various variables that are being utilized to determine if a piece of data is relevant or not are often less black and white than those that a computer program could determine.

Furthermore, the points that are subject to cleaning are typically dramatic outliers of the data that you have collected. This means that they do not fit the flow of the other data that you have collected, often by being at one far end of the spectrum of data or the other. Determining which points are outliers is as easy as plotting the data and then looking for the points that are far away from the majority of the spread of data points. Alternatively, you can first run an analysis on the data in question before cutting out those points that are outside of the control limits that were set during the analysis. You can then remove those points and redo the analysis in order to get more accurate results.

The importance of having the cleanest, and therefore the most useful data possible cannot be overstated. It is common for analysts, especially those new to the field, to become somewhat lost in the complexity of the data that they are working with and the methods that are being used to analyze them. This, in turn, can easily lead to results that point in a misleading direction, causing hardship and potential financial ruin in the process. A good rule of thumb is that when you are analyzing statistics you are going to want to spend about 80 percent of your time ensuring that the data has been cleaned properly and the remaining 20 percent actually doing analysis.

## Data visualization

Sometimes just referred to as visualization, data visualization is all about creating visual representations of the data that you have discovered in an effort to not only explain the data in question, but also make it easier for anyone to understand. This is often done through things like statistical or informational graphics or by plotting data. Bars, lines and dots are all commonly used when it comes to visualizing numbers in an effort to make various hidden trends more visible. As it is not limited by the traditional confines of communicated information, a properly developed visualization will make it easier to find and explore new insights as well as understand the story that the data is trying to tell.

## Making Effective Graphs

When it comes to graphing the information that you have found in an effective way, it is important to keep in mind the type of graphics that you will use in an effort to get to the heart of the data. In order to do that you are going to want to, first and foremost, show off the data in the most effective way possible by introducing those who look at the data to the substance of what it is you have been doing, not all the precise technical work that made it happen. Additionally, it is important to keep in mind that whatever you do, you are going to want to avoid accidentally distorting the data by presenting it in a misleading way.

Above all though, it is important that a good graph presents a large amount of numerical data in a small space that remains coherent, even when viewed from a large scale. It should also naturally lead viewers to compare various pieces of relevant data based on how it is arranged, and in so doing show the viewer data at numerous different levels of overall detail. You will also want it to be clear in its exploration, description, and purpose.

If you choose to go against these time-honored principles, then you are courting disaster in the form of misleading graphs which support actions that might very well be disastrous if followed through to their logical conclusion. *Chartjunk* is the phrase that is used to describe extraneous frills that novice analysts frequently add to their graphs in an effort to give them a little style or personality. This practice should be discouraged, however, as you don't want anything taking the focus away from the numbers, their trends, and their relative importance.

Additionally, you are going to want to avoid adding anything that does not directly enhance the message the data is putting forth. This goes for separating related information so that the viewer has to keep turning their head back and forth in a gratuitous fashion as well; you want to cut down on everything that obscures the data in any way. Remember, when making a chart you are going to want to ensure that the amount of ink you use should be as minimal as possible while still transmitting the maximum amount of data possible.

## Commonly Graphed Information

There are eight primary types of information, sometimes called messages, that can be communicated via the data that you find, and each has a commonly used graph to make that message as clear as possible.

*Time Series:* In a time series, a single variable is going to be captured over a prolonged period of time. They are typically visualized with the use of a line chart in order to demonstrate their trend clearly. A good example of a time series is when the unemployment rate is tracked over a prolonged period of time.

*Ranking:* Typically done in either ascending or descending order, this information places categorical subdivisions in order based on an external, unbiased fashion. They are commonly represented by a bar chart which can be used to easily compare several different variables at once. A common use of a ranking system is when sales performance, which is being measured, is broken down by individual sales people, the categorical subdivision.

*Part-to-whole:* Typically, categorical subdivisions are measured in terms of ratio and the whole, generally in terms of percent out of 100. They are typically visualized via the use of a bar chart or a pie chart in an effort to making comparing various ratios as easy as possible. A common use for this type of visualization is the various market shares that certain competitors hold in a given marketplace.

*Deviation:* Categorical subdivisions can also be compared to a third party reference, as is often the case for things like budgeted for expenses versus the actual cost of expenses in a given timeframe. A bar chart is typically used in this scenario for the ease with which it can show comparisons between the two amounts in question.

*Frequency Distribution:* A frequency distribution is commonly used to indicate the number of times a particular was observed in a given period of time. The type of bar chart known as a histogram is typically considered the most useful type of graph to represent this type of analysis. Additionally, a boxplot can be useful when it comes to visualizing various statistics related to distribution including things like outlier, quartiles and median. Frequency distribution is commonly used for tasks such as determining the number of years a specific stock market return fell with a specific range.

*Correlation:* A correlation is useful when you need to compare observations related to two different variables for the purpose of deciding if they are likely to move in the same or the opposite direction. A scatter plot is generally considered the best choice when it comes to conveying this type of information. A common use for this type of visualization is determining how inflation and unemployment numbers track off of one another for a set period of months.

*Nominal comparison:* A nominal comparison is useful when you need to compare numerous categorical subdivisions but you aren't particularly picky when it comes to the order that they are in. A bar chart is the type of graph typically used when doing those types of comparisons and they are especially useful when graphing things like product code or sales volume.

*Geospatial or Geographic:* A geospatial or geographic visualization is useful when you are interested in comparing variables as they change over a physical space. This type of comparison is typically done via the use of a cartogram and can be used for things like determining the property tax in different areas of a state.

All told, when you are reviewing data, it is important to keep in mind the various ways that such data is commonly presented, and if one or more of the above visualizations is the right choice for the patterns that you feel are revealing themselves in the data that you are studying. If you find yourself in a scenario where there are multiple different variations of the data that seem to make sense when it comes to telling the type of story you are interested in telling, then the best thing to do is to simply generate both the visualizations in question and see which one expresses the message you are looking to convey in the simplest and most direct way possible.

# Data Prediction Techniques-Regression

There are many different techniques and variations on approaches that can be used when it comes to conducting predictive analysis properly. Primarily, these can be either machine learning technique or regression techniques, with regression techniques taking up the focus of this chapter and machine learning the next. Of the two, regression models are definitively the more important of the two as well, with many analysts considering them the mainstay of effective predictive analytics. The key to this fact lies in the focus they bring to establishing a relevant mathematical model that accurately represents what is taking place between the variables you are actively keeping track of. While there are numerous different models that can be used, the most common ones are explained below.

## Linear Regression

Linear regression is the most common, and therefore one of the most useful types of predictive analysis that you will come across. In this case, regression estimates prove to be a useful way of describing data in a way that gives proper credence to the relationship between a pair of variables that you are tracking. The heart of this type of regression analysis lies with the task of finding a way to make a single line fit throughout a scatter plot.

The easiest way of doing this is with a single dependent variable, as well as a single independent variable, in a way that can be explained via the formula $y=c+b*x$. In this scenario, $y$ is equal to the estimated dependent variable, $c$ is going to be equal to the constant that you are working with, *b* will be equal to the coefficient regression and *x* will equal the variable that is independent.

In this instance, it is also possible for the dependent variable to also be referred to as the regressand, the prognostic variable, the endogenous variable or even the criterion variable. Meanwhile, the independent variable can also be referred to as either the regressor, the predictor variable or the exogenous variable.

There is more to analysis of linear regression than simply finding the best way for a line to move through a scatter plot however; specifically, three different stages that will need to be completed every time you are hoping to use this type of regression to find potential insight into the future. In the first stage, you are going to want to analyze the directionality as well as any correlation that the data might provide. Then you are going to want to estimate the model by fitting the line appropriately, and finally you are going to want to evaluate how useful and accurate the resulting model really is.

There are three main types of use that you will find for this type of regression analysis, the first of which is causal analysis when you are more interested in getting a general idea about what it is you are working with and less interested in being as accurate as you possibly can. You will also find it useful when you are looking to forecast a specific type of effect or trend.

While doing so, it is important to keep in mind that this type of analysis assumes that there is a causal relationship or a dependence between an independent variable and a dependent variable. This type of regression analysis can also determine the relative strength of the effect that the variables have on one another. If this is the type of relationship that you are looking for, then while looking through your data you are going to want to ask yourself what the current relationship between things like age on income, sales and marketing budgets or doses and various effects is.

## Time Series Analysis

The need for time series analysis typically arises most frequently when there is a need to monitor business metrics or to track industrial processes. Specifically, it is useful when it comes to taking into account the innate fact about data points when taken over time, specifically the fact that they have an internal structure that can be accounted for with enough data. To that end, a time series is a sequence of values that are ordered in a period of time intervals that are equally spaced. As such, time series analysis has proven useful in numerous different applications including census analysis, utility studies, workload projection, inventory studies, process and quality control, yield projections, stock market analysis, budgetary analysis, sales forecasting and economic forecasting, among others.

*Important techniques:* Ensuring that a time series model fits the data that is being provided can sometimes be a complicated task. Luckily, there are numerous modeling methods that can be used to make things easier, the most common of which, known as the Box Jenkins modeling methods, will be discussed in detail shortly. First, however, it is important to have a clear idea of the basic techniques related to smoothing that come into play for this type of model.

Smoothing techniques, sometimes also called moving average techniques, are a method of minimizing the amount of random variation that is inherent in nearly all types of data collection. When applied properly, smoothing can make an underlying trend, be it cyclical or seasonal, much more apparent. Smoothing can further be broken down into two different types, the first of which is known as the averaging method. As the name implies, in the averaging method you simply take a sample of total data that you have previously collected and then find the average based on the variables that you are tracking.

Next, you are then going to want to determine if the average estimate you came up with is likely to be accurate or not using what is known as the mean squared error. Finding the mean squared error is a reliable way of determining if your model is going to be reliable or not. To find it, you start by finding the error amount, specifically the average result, subtracted by the real result. You will then want to square the amount. Additionally, you will want to find the sum of the squared errors as well as the mean of all of the squared errors that you find. Finally, you will want to determine which estimate had the small mean of all squared errors, as this is the estimate that is the closest to reality overall.

However, it is important to keep in mind that the mean that has been found in relation to past observations is only ever going to be a useful tool when it comes to forecasting the future when there are no other trends available. If trends are available, then they are likely going to be a better indicator of future likelihoods. Additionally, you will want to remember that the past weighs all instances of occurrence equally, which is not always going to be the case in the instances you are measuring.

*Box Jenkins Model:* The modeling programs that are discussed in chapter 10 can be utilized to create a Box Jenkins model with time series data that you have collected. There are several things that you need to keep in mind when using this type of model, however, including that the model assumes that the time series in question is going to be stationary. Non-stationary series can be made stationary by simply differencing them at least once. Additionally, you will need to be aware that certain formulations are known to cause a transformation in the series by reducing each data point by the mean of the series beforehand. This, in turn, will yield a series with an overall mean that is zero. This is not required in all software models.

Box Jenkins models can also be extended in such a way that they are able to include seasonal autoregressive as well terms that are moving average. While this can make the process more complicated, the concepts at the heart of both terms are similar however, and will still be based on averaging moving terms. It is also possible for this model to include seasonal autoregressive terms, difference operators and moving average terms. That doesn't mean they should always be included, however, and the best choice is to always only focus on the terms you are the most interested in.

*Creating a Box Jenkins model:* When it comes to creating your own Box-Jenkins model, the first thing you are going to need to do is to determine how much seasonality you are going to need to factor into your model or if it is more of a stationary measurement. You can detect the given level of stationarity by using a run sequence plot to determine how constant the scale and location of your data is going to be. With that in mind you are going to want to determine the order and any seasonal autoregressive terms if they exist.

In many instances, these series will include a clearly defined period which means that only one seasonality term will be required. While you will not need to necessarily remove this seasonality to fit the model properly, you will want to ensure the seasonal terms are ordered properly in your software. With that out of the way, you are then going to want to find the moving average terms as well as the autoregressive terms. The best ways for doing so are through finding the autocorrelation plot as well as a partial version of the same. The sample plots are then matched to the theoretical plots to determine what behavior is actually known.

For a basic process, the autocorrelation function will need to appear exponentially decreasing. If it is process of a higher order, however, then you will want to find a mix of sinusoidal components that are decreasing. In this instance you will be able to use the autocorrelation to determine if there is a variance in the departure from zero. The best way to do this is to indicate that you have approximately 95 percent confidence in the sample that you have created. If the end result results in a decay towards zero then you will know that it is going to be an autoregressive model; if the shape ends up alternating between positive and negative, then you will know that it is going to be an autoregressive model as well. However, if one of spikes and the remainder are all exactly at zero then you know you are looking at a moving average model. Meanwhile, if you notice decay after a few lags have already happened then you know, you are looking at a mixed autoregressive model that is also a moving average.

Enjoying your eBook so far? Take a moment to subscribe to our FREE newsletter for incredible discounts, books giveaways, and VIP offers!

> ➢ http://www.connectionbooksclub.com/bonus/

All we need is your email, and you'll be set up to receive more of the eBooks you can't wait to read.

# Data Prediction Techniques-Machine Learning

Machine learning in general is considered a branch of artificial intelligence and it was first created as a basic way to allow computers to learn. With the wide variety of complicated methods of statistical analysis that are available today, this type of learning can also be used for a wide variety of things including stock market analysis, speech or face recognition, fraud detection and even medical diagnostics. What's more, given the right variables, it can accurately predict future variables without directly dealing with the relationships that underlie the effect that certain variables have on one another. Alternatively, it can be used to accurately pinpoint relationships that otherwise might seem too complex to map accurately. In this cases, the machine learning techniques that are being called into play actually successfully match patterns present in human cognition which means that it is learning from the past in order to predict the future.

## Neural Networks

An artificial neural network can be thought of as a type of processor that is made up of layers, with each layer, in turn, being made up of different nodes. Each node then contains what is known as an activation function which then triggers it to flip in the presence of certain types of patterns. Furthermore, the network as a whole is made up of code that allows it to learn based on the information it has been provided. The result of this learning is that some nodes are prioritized over others when it comes to making decisions because they have been proven to be more relevant to results that have occurred in the past.

While there are several different types of learning rules available, by far, the most common is known as the delta rule. When using the delta rule, learning occurs in cycles that take place each time a new pattern is detected. The first time that the pattern is detected, the network will guess as to what the outcome is going to be, it then cycles and sees if its results were accurate, and if not, how inaccurate they actually were. Using the actual results as well as the estimated results, it then retries a new hypothesis and repeats the cycle as needed.

Due to the fact that the specifics of the space or margin of error is impossible to deduce ahead of time, it is common for analysis done via a neural network to take a significant number of tests, called runs, in order to come up with what is likely to be the most effective solution moving forward. This speed can be adjusted through what are known as mathematical assist terms. This will help the network build a steady momentum and reach a reliable answer more quickly.

After a neural network has reached a level where it has a clear idea of what is going on in regards to a given problem, it can then be given additional types of data to work with. This can be done by forcing the network to work in propagation mode moving forward. This will ensure that new inputs are factored through the lens of prior inputs and are not simply replacing them.

When pursuing this course of action, it is important to keep in mind that a neural network can be trained to exhaustively regard a certain type of input that it becomes unreliable when used with any other types of input. This is referred to as being *grandmothered*, and is guaranteed to leave your neural network practically useless.

## Multilayer Perceptron Neural Network

The multilayer perceptron model is a type of neural networking model that matches relevant inputs with related outputs. It is comprised of numerous layers of nodes set up so that its vertices are connected by the edges, but each edge has a specific direction it is associated with as well. Each of these layers is then connected fully to the ones on either side of it. Additionally, while the input node is different, the remainder of the nodes can be thought of as neuron, or processing core, with a specific activation function, just like in a more traditional neural network. It is superior to the more common type of neural network as it is capable of more clearly distinguishing data that is not separable in a linear way.

It is this ability to consider activation functions that are nonlinear as well as the more common linear options that are available in a more traditional neural network. This allows it to determine the frequency of action potentials in much the same way that neurons fire in your own brain. This idea can be expressed through the activation function that can be written as $y(v_i)=\tanh(v_i)$ as well as $y(v_i)=1+e^{-v1})^{-1}$. In this case, $y$ is going to be the output of the ith node while $v_i$ can be thought of as the sum of the input after it has been appropriately weighted. There are other types of activation functions that can be used including radial basis function, soft plus function and rectified functions.

The phrase multilayer perceptron can be confusing to some people because the model can be considered, not as a single perceptron with many layers, but instead as a group of perceptron working in layers towards a group goal. What's more, these groupings of perceptrons aren't even true perceptrons in the traditional sense as they aren't bound to a single activation function but are instead free to take that which makes the most sense in the moment.

Through the use of the same type of back-propagation algorithm that can be seen in a standard neural network, multilayer perceptrons can be found as part of the standard analysis algorithm for pattern recognition processes around the world, though they are especially useful when it comes to parallel distributed processing and computational neuroscience. They are also found in research where the data is particularly difficult to approximate successfully as is the case with things like approximating someone's overall level of fitness. Additionally, they are known to function as universal approximators, which means they are useful when it comes to creating models that are based on types of regression analysis. They can also be used as a type of classification for regression if the response is likely to be categorical.

## Support Vector Machine

When it comes to machine learning, a support vector machine is a type of supervised learning model which uses a variety of algorithms associated with learning in an effort to analyze data for easier use with either regression analysis or classification. When a support vector machine is given a group of examples for the purpose of training, then each is marked as belonging to one of a pair of categories which, in turn, makes it easier to classify future objects into one of the categories. This makes it what is known as a binary linear classifier of the non-probalistic variety.

Once it is fully generated, a support vector machine model is a visual representation of numerous points in space but mapped in such a way that the categories that have been defined are clearly separated from one another via a gap that you will want to be as large as possible. From there, when new examples are added to the model, it will generate a predication as to what side of the gap it is going to fall on.

What's more, support vector machines are known to be able to effectively classify in a non-linear way as well, through the use of something known as feature space that is high dimensional. This means that a support vector machine can also be used effectively if the data you are working with has not previously been tested and labeled properly. In these instances, it can use what is known as an unsupervised learning approach which allows it to look at the way the data in question groups naturally before mapping additional data to these various groups as it is acquired. This ability is what is known as support vector clustering and is most commonly used in industrial settings where it can be difficult to ensure that data is labeled properly as it is generated.

Specifically, the support vector machines that you will be likely working with are constructed using at least one hyperplane that is located in a dimensional space that is infinite, or at least high. It can then be used for tasks like regression or classification as the separation between data will occur naturally and will be visible as the hyperplane that has the greatest amount of distance between itself and a local training data point or functional margin. Remember, the larger the margin is, the lower the overall classifier generalization error is going to be.

**Naïve Bayes Classifier**

In machine learning it is important to be able to construct classifiers, more specifically, class labels that are assigned by models which are drawn from a predetermined list of classifiers. It is not just one algorithm but a variety of algorithms that share one thing in common. Specifically, they assume that the value of a feature is not related to the value of any other features related to that same variable. On the contrary, a naïve Bayes classifier will consider each feature for what it contributes independently to the overall probability of the question in question without worry about correlations between the individual features.

While some probability model types can be naturally trained using naïve Bayes classifiers via a supervised learning session, it will often be difficult in practice as the parameter estimation that is often used in models made using the naïve Bayes method which focuses on the maximum likelihood of an event happening instead. While this type of classification and assumption may seem oversimplified, they traditionally prove quite successful in real-world settings time and again. One of the reasons it remains so effective is that it requires relatively little regarding training data before parameters of effect can begin to be estimated.

While the more far-reaching of naïve Bayes assumptions can prove inaccurate, there are several other properties that prove it is useful in many scenarios. Specifically, when it comes to decoupling class conditional distribution of features, a naïve Bayes can be used to properly determine the distribution element by simply estimated each as a dimensional distribution with only one dimension. Doing so can help prevent problems from occurring when it comes to more complicated types of dimensionality, specifically the need for sets of data to scale properly with the number of features that are currently being explored.

Despite the fact that a naïve Bayes is often known to fail when it comes to producing accurate class probability estimates, this is not actually a requirement for all applications, which means it can still be extremely useful as long as you take its limitations into account. Instead, it is perfectly acceptable for the naïve Bayes to instead make the appropriate decision based on classification of which classification is most likely, even if there are no other classification options available to it. This will also be true no matter if the probability is inaccurate, no matter if the degree to which it is inaccurate is vast or microscopic. As such, the overall classifier can still be soundly robust enough that it has the ability to shrug off major deficiencies related to the naïve probability model that it underlines.

Enjoying your eBook so far? Take a moment to subscribe to our FREE newsletter for incredible discounts, books giveaways, and VIP offers!

> http://www.connectionbooksclub.com/bonus/

All we need is your email, and you'll be set up to receive more of the eBooks you can't wait to read.

# Utilizing Discrete Choice Models

Discrete choice modeling is also known as qualitative choice modeling, but whatever name you think of it as, it is always a type of predictive analysis that aims to determine the types of choices existing customers are going to make when it comes to choosing certain products and services over other competing products and services. The idea here is that by identifying the patterns that underlie these various choices, discrete choice models can then determine why consumers respond to different products in different ways. Discrete choice models also allow marketers to take a closer look at the impact of things like amount of promotion, pricing, service bundling and product configuration when it comes to market share and mindshare among different types of consumers.

The theory at play behind discrete choice models is that every purchase that a customer makes is a conscious choice. These choices include not just which product to purchase in general and which brand to purchase specifically, but also whether or not they are going to buy right this minute, at a point later on, or if they are going to reject the decision to buy anything at all. While some of the reasoning behind these types of decisions can be extremely complex and difficult to pin down the specifics on, there are typically enough variables that you can count on that you can effectively make fairly accurate generalizations based on key information.

To think of it another way, consider what would happen if you flipped a coin. While in general you will never be able to tell if the coin is going to land heads or tails on any individual flip, you would be able to predict that it is going to end up heads about 50 percent of the time and tails the other 50 percent. The same is true with consumers, while an individual might always surprise you, there is a lot you can accurately predict about an individual simply by knowing a few key characteristics. Specifically, you are going to want to keep in mind the details of the product in question, its price and the social and economic characteristics the consumer displays.

**Using a discrete choice model**

*Getting Started:* In order to use a discrete choice model effectively, the first thing you are going to want to do is to utilize the information gathering method of focus groups in order to properly identify the key buying factors related to the product that you are interested in gathering more data on. These groups will help to explore the motivations that your consumers have in greater detail while at the same time allowing you to develop a relevant hypothesis in terms of what motivates choice regarding the type of product in question.

*Determining Preferences:* From there, the next step is going to be testing the hypothesis that you have formed through an experimental setting. Specifically, this step can go in two different directions, though you will be using surveys regardless. The first direction involves working with an existing product and considering how to improve it. In this option you create a survey for potential customers regarding their buying habits or thoughts on future purchases in the general category relating to product that you are trying to market.

These types of surveys are often called revealed preference studies and they are especially useful when used with products that already exist as they are a great way to determine the current conditions the market is facing. Due to the current nature of the research you are also less likely to find a discrepancy between what customers intend to buy and what their actual purchase behaviors truly are.

Alternatively, if you are still working out the specifics of the product you may instead find it useful to offer a survey to potential customers in the form of a series of choice experiments. With each, you would present the potential customer with a pair of products and then see what they pick, you will also want to take note if they choose to buy one of the products now, buy neither of the products or indicate that they would likely buy one of the products at a later time.

You will also want to ask about each pair of products while varying different important characteristics such as pricing and availability to see if anything changes. These types of surveys are often referred to as state preference studies and if you carefully choose the options that the potential customers have to choose from, then you can ultimately get a very accurate feel as to how certain segments of the market view various types of tradeoffs when it comes to relevant prices and product requirements.

When it comes to new products you are going to be limited to state preference studies assuming that there are no products on the market currently that can be an adequate stand in for the product that you are planning to develop. If the product that you are intending to study does already exist, then you will instead want to start with state preference experiments and then see how they compare to the revealed preference data that you will also want to collect. Doing so will help you to make sure that the resulting discrete choice models don't track purchasing intention but rather actual purchasing behavior.

*Building a model:* After you have collected all the data that you feel is going to be relevant to the model in question, the final step is to actually go ahead and build the model in question. Programs for doing so are discussed in chapter 10, though you will need to answer some questions before you get started in order to see the best results. These questions include things like:

- What are the most important segments of the market for this item to see success in?
- How price sensitive are those markets?
- Are brand names a factor for the type of product?
- What type of advertising is going to find the most success?
- Where will targeted efforts yield the most results?

## Benefits of a Discrete Choice Model

Conducting these types of experiments can yield a wide variety of advantages, the most important of which being that you are in no way limited in terms of attributes and scenarios that exist in the real market which can be useful if you are more interested in getting in on the ground floor of a new trend rather than playing catchup with something that already exists on the market. These sorts of things can include advertising, promotion, effects, shelf space, performance, perceived quality, brand impact and product style among others.

Additionally, it will allow you to manipulate various additional aspects of the design in an effort to ensure you get a wide variety of input about various price points and feature sets from a wide variety of different types of people. The information that you gained in the first step of this process will help you get started in terms of choosing a primary target audience while the second step is useful for testing the information you found in the first step more stringently.

Furthermore, these types of studies are known to create two different types of deliverables. The first of these is going to be a report that allows you to see marketing recommendations based on the information that the discrete choice models uncovered. Additionally, you will be able to see a simulation that lets you toggle various hypothetical instances where you can see a prediction of what is likely to happen if the product is released at several different prices or with various marketing strategies.

When it comes to using the results as effectively as possible, the first thing you are going to want to keep in mind is that discrete choice model study results can typically be applied to one of two main categories decisions made in relation to tactical marketing or strategic planning applications. Strategic planning applications are things that tend to involve a direct plan of action. This can include things like identifying factors that are critical to success when it comes to a new product or service, finding a likely amount of market interest in regards to a new product or service, determining how the market is going to be segmented based on various factors, and determining likely levels of demand in various regions. On the other hand, tactical marketing applications tend to involve doing things with a specific end goal in mind including things like determining adequate services and products in response to new opportunities or threats in an existing marketplace, finding the optimum pricing plan for a given product, positioning a product properly in comparison to its competitors and determining the current value of a product's brand or determining when it is time to rebrand a product.

## Additional Considerations

When it comes to planning to create a discrete choice model, the first thing you are going to need to consider is the amount of time it can take to act on effectively. First you need to consider the amount of time it takes to run a single focus group and then take into account that you may need to run several, especially if you are starting fresh and coming up with a new product. Alternatively, if you are in a hurry to see results you can limit the sample time, and thus the amount of time required, though this is not recommended.

After that, you are going to need to factor in the amount of time it is going to take to create the various surveys that you are going to want to use, as well as the time it is going to take to collect the required information and then clean it to ensure it is at its most useful. Finally, you will need to consider the amount of time it will take you to create your actual models so that they are as useful as possible. All told, you can expect for this process to take at least five weeks, though if it is the first time that you are creating a discrete choice model then you can expect it to take up to twice as long because it will likely take you several tries to get the results you are looking for as you streamline your focus group and surveying process.

In addition to the time considerations that you are going to want to account for, the other thing you are going to want to keep in mind is that if you are planning to create a discrete choice model for a new product, then you are going to need to budget a minimum of $25,000 for the process. While it can be cheaper if you are working on pivoting an existing product, brand-new products are likely going to require multiple focus groups, and the average cost for a focus group tends to run close to $5,000. Again, you can always choose to limit your sample size, and thus your costs, but doing so risks limiting your effectiveness as well. If money is the biggest issue, your best bet might be to hold off until you can afford to do it properly as creating discrete choice models as a half measure can easily lead to skewed results.

Once you have made it through the data gathering phase, you will then need to determine how you want to proceed with the quantitative phase where you can easily determine how precise you want the information you collect to be, versus the relative cost of collecting it. Remember, the larger the sample size, the greater the cost but the more useful the data will turn out to be. The scope and nature of the discrete choice model that you are creating will have some say over these parameters, but you will still have a fair degree of control over the ultimate costs and results.

While the costs can be high, it is important to keep in mind that the return on investment is typically considered quite robust as well. To wit, a return of at least ten times the amount that is spent on discrete choice model creation is considered common, while returns of up to one hundred times the initial investment are known to occur on occasion.

# Data Management Mistakes to Avoid

*Choosing a data warehouse based on what you need in the moment:* With all the myriad of steps that come with setting up your data stream so that it is effective in the present, it can be easy to not think about the long term when it comes to choosing the data warehouse that is right for you. This is a folly, however, as making long-term data decision with only the short term in mind is an easy way to ensure that a few years down the line you are going to be cursing the limitations you accidentally imposed on yourself.

This means that if you want the future in your favor, you will want to look at least three, but as many as five, years down the road in terms of where you want your company to be at that time and what you expect for your overall needs and requirements to be at that time as well. Don't forget to focus as much on the technical aspects of what you will need as well as the business strategy you will be using.

*Considering metadata as an afterthought:* While it might seem like something you can easily go back and tinker with at a later date, failing to make the right meta data choices early on can have long reaching and disastrous implications in the long term. Instead of thinking of it as an afterthought, you should consider it to be the key integrator when it comes to making different types of data models play nice with one another. This means you will want to consider long-term data requirements when making your choices and also document everything along the way.

To do this properly you will want to start by ensuring that every column and table that you create has its own descriptions and key phrases. It is amazing how many problems you can quickly and easily solve in the long term by simply picking a labeling and naming convention early on and sticking with it throughout your time with the data warehouse.

*Underestimate the usefulness of ad hoc querying:* While generating a simple report seems as though it should be, for lack of a better word, simple, in reality it can easily expand considerably, causing bandwidth costs to skyrocket and productivity to decrease overall due to the extra strain. This issue can be avoided by simply relying on the metadata layer to create the reports instead. This will make things go much more smoothly without directly affecting the secure and sanctified nature of the underlying data. This can also make it easier for less knowledgeable users to get where they need to and interact with the system appropriately which, in turn, can make it easier for it to gain a wider amount of buy in from key individuals.

*Letting for supersede function:* When it comes to deciding on a reporting layer for the data warehouse that you are ultimately going to, hopefully, be using for years to come, you may be tempted to pick something that is visually appealing, without really considering the long-term implications of what that decision can mean. Specifically, it is important that you don't choose a visual presentation style that causes the system to run slower than it otherwise would. To understand why even a five second difference in load time can be a huge time waster, take a minute to consider how frequently this system is going to be used and by how many people. With so many multipliers it won't take long for five seconds to become hours, if not days.

In addition to saving you and your team time, speedier systems will also make it more likely for various team members to actively participate with the system because its ease of use will be greater, if not necessarily prettier. Additionally, the faster that data can be generated, the more likely it is to remain true to the source, which will ensure you have a higher overall quality of data to work with than you otherwise might.

*Focusing on cleaning data after it has already been stored:* Once your data warehouse is up and running, you are going to want to ensure any data that you actually put into it is going to be as accurate and as clean as possible. There are multiple reasons that this is the right choice, the first of which is that team members are much more likely to actually fill out relevant information in regards to topics the business cares about, as well as notice errors right away as opposed to at a later date. Additionally, the old adage that once something is out of sight, it is out of mind as well, is just as true with data as it is with anything else. As such, even if team members have the best intentions when it comes to data, after it has been filed away it is much easier to forget about it and move on to another task.

While the occasional piece of unfiltered data slipping through isn't going to affect things all that much, if too much unfiltered data gets through then the data as a whole is much more likely to find discrepancies when compared with what actually happened. Remember, the longer that a warehouse continues to collect data, the larger the number of inaccurate pieces of information it has collected will be. This doesn't necessarily mean that there is anything wrong with the current system, these sorts of this happen naturally as a result of humans being a part of the process at all. That doesn't mean you want to add more issues to pile, however, which is what makes cleaning the data first and foremost so important.

The best preventative measure when it comes to error-ridden data is to include some sort of active monitoring system in the data management system that you use. Quality control can also be governed by common usage as well as the data coherence plan that your business already has in place.

*Allowing data warehouse tasks to be purely the concern of those in IT:* While those in the IT department are likely going to be a great source of valid knowledge when it comes to implementing your own data warehouse, it is important that they do not control the entirety of the project. Rather, you will want to keep in mind that those who are going to be the point of entry for most of the data are likely going to be the ones who utilize the system most frequently which, in turn, means that they should be consulted when it comes to key features to ensure that the system is not dead in the water within six months because a crucial feature for your team is especially difficult to use.

*Treating only certain types of data as relevant:* When you are first starting out it can be easy to visualize Big Data as just that, big, and uniform, and able to fit easily into a one-size-fits-all bin. The reality is that Big Data actually comes in a variety of shapes and sizes as well as in three primary groups. Each of these groups is especially relevant to a certain sector of business and you will need to know how you plan on using all of them if you hope to create a successful management system.

Data can be unstructured, which means it is likely images, audio or video, though simple text can also be unstructured. On the other hand, data can be structured which includes thinks like mathematical models, risk models, financial models, actuarial modes, sensor data and machine data. Finally, in-between is the semi-structured data which includes things like software modules, spreadsheets, earnings reports and emails.

*Focusing on data quantity over quality:* With Big Data on everyone's minds and lips, it can be easy to get so focused on obtaining as much information as possible that quantity of data ends up mattering more than the quality of the data that you collect. This is a big mistake, however, as data of a low quality, even if it has been cleaned can still skew analytics in unwanted ways. This means that not only is it important to know how to process Big Data effectively and to seek out the most useful and relevant information possible at each and every opportunity; it is also extremely important to understand how to improve the quality of data that is being collected in the first place.

When it comes to unstructured data, it is important to note that if you are interested in improving the quality of the data that is being collected, this should be done by improving the libraries that are used for language correction prior to the data being uploaded to the warehouse. If translation is required, then it is best to have a human hand in that process as the finer points of translation are still lost in most cases on automatic translation programs. When it comes to semi-structured data with either numeric or text values, it is important to run it through the same process of correction that you would more traditional text files. Additionally, you are going to need to plan for lots of user input to make sure the data comes out the other side in its most useful and accurate state. Structured data should generally be in a useful state already and should not require further effort.

*Failing to think about granularity:* Once again, because of its lumbering nature, it is easy for those who are just getting started with analytics to create a data warehouse without taking into account the level of granularity that will ultimately be required from the data in question. While you won't be able to determine exactly how granular you are going to need to go up-front, you are going to want to be aware of the fact that it will eventually be required and plan for it in the construction phase. Failing to do so can leave you with an inability to process the relevant metrics that you are interested in, as well as leaving you foggy on their relevant hierarchies and related metrics. The situation can grow out of control extremely quickly, especially when you are working with either semi-structured or text-based data. As these are the two types of data that you are going to come into contact with the most, it is definitely worth giving some early consideration.

*Contextualizing incorrectly:* While it is important to contextualize the data that you collect, it is going to be equally important to contextualize it in the right way for later use. Not only will this make the data more useful in the long term when the original details have largely faded away, it will also reduce the potential risk of inaccuracy that brings with it an increased chance of skewed analytics further down the line. Especially, dealing with text that comes from multiple businesses or multiple disciplines, it is important that you always plan to have a knowledgeable human on hand to ensure that this information makes it into the data warehouse in a manner that is not only useful, but also as accurate as possible. Finally, contextualizing is important because, when tagged correctly, it can make it easier to pepper the database with additional interconnected topics.

Enjoying your eBook so far? Take a moment to subscribe to our FREE newsletter for incredible discounts, books giveaways, and VIP offers!

- http://www.connectionbooksclub.com/bonus/

All we need is your email, and you'll be set up to receive more of the eBooks you can't wait to read.

# Starter Software to Collect Data

While there are certainly plenty of commercial predictive analytic software on the market today, there are also plenty of free, open source products available that you can get started with right now, for no money down. While the following list will give you a good place to start, if you don't see the type of software that you are looking for here, odds are a quick online search will be able to point you in the right direction.

*Apache Mahout:* Created by the Apache Software foundation, Apache Mahout is a free scalable algorithm related to machine learning and primarily focused on classification, clustering and collaborative filtering. It also allows users to access common Java libraries for help when it comes to common math operations including things like statistics and linear algebra. It also offers access to primitive Java collections as well for those who need to use them instead.

The algorithms that it uses for filtering, classification and clustering have all been implemented based around the Apache Hadoop reduce/map paradigm. It in no way restricts this implementation and any contributions that use only a single node or other type of cluster can be used as well. As of September 2016, this is still a relatively new product which means that while it has a wide variety of algorithms already available, there are still gaps in what it can and cannot offer. Apache Mahout can be found online for free at mahout.apache.org. Apache Mahout does not require Apache Hadoop in order to function properly.

*GNU Octave:* GNU Octave is a program language software designed for high-level use. It was originally designed to help with complicated numerical computations of both the nonlinear and linear variety as well as other similar numerical based experiments. It primarily utilizes a batch-oriented language that is largely compatible with MATLAB as well. It was created as part of the GNU Project which means that it is a free software by default based on the GNU General Public License. The fact that it is generally compatible with MATLAB is noteworthy because Octave is the primary free competitor to MATLAB.

Notable GNU Octave features include the ability to type a TAB character using the command line in order to force Octave to try and complete the file name, function or variable in question. It does this using the text prior to where the cursor is location as a baseline for what needs to be completed. You can also look into your command history as well as organize your data structures to a limited degree. Furthermore, GNU Octave uses logical short-circuit Boolean type operators which are then evaluated in the way that a short circuit would be. Other operators include both decrement operators as well as increment operators available in both a postfix and a prefix form which helps it also deal with augmented assignment issues. It also offers a limited form of support for exception handling that is based on the idea of unwind and protect. GNU Octave is available online at GNU.org/Software/Octave.

*KNIME:* Also known as the Konstanz Information Miner, KNIME is a platform that focuses on integration, reporting and data analytics. Furthermore, it uses different components of various other tasks including data mining and machine learning through a unique pipeline based on modular data. It also boasts a graphical user interface which makes creating the nodes that are then used in data preprocessing a much less complicated process. KNIME is mainly used in the medical field though it has been expanding in the past decade and can also be useful when it comes to analyzing financial data, business intelligence and customer data.

It works by letting users create visual data flows, which it calls pipeline, while also letting them then selectively execute one or more in the steps of the actual analysis as well as inspect the various results, views and models that have been created. KNIME is based on the Java platform using Eclipse and it also utilizes an extension in an effort to add plugins for a greater array of functionality than what the base program can offer. The free version includes more than 200 modules that of options when it comes to data visualization, data analysis, data transformation, database management and data integration. Using the additional extension available for free to design reports, you can even use KNIME reports to automatically generate a wide variety of clear and informative charts as well. KINE can be found online, for free, at KNIME.org.

*Open NM:* The Open Neural Networks Library, OPEN NM for short is a C++ software library and is licensed under the GNU Lesser General Public License which means it is free to those who use it in good faith. Overall, it can be thought of as a software package containing a general purpose artificial intelligence system. It then uses typical techniques seen in machine learning as a way of successfully executing on predictive analysis and data mining problems that otherwise may be too complex to master with any true degree of certainty. This software is useful in that it combines numerous layers of processing units in a nonlinear fashion with the goal of increasing supervised learning.

Furthermore, its unique architecture allows it to work with neural networks which contain properties of universal approximation. Furthermore, it allows for programming via multiprocessing means such as OpenMP for those interested in increasing computational performance.

OpenNN also uses data mining algorithms that come bundled as functions. These can then be eventually embedded in other tools and software of your choosing using the including interface for application programming. When used properly, this makes it much easier than it might otherwise be to find new ways to integrate predictive analysis into even more tasks. Take note, it does not offer a traditional graphical interface but some visualization tools do support it. OpenNN is available online, for free, at OpenNN.net

*Orange Software:* Orange Software is a free type of data mining software that is written in the popular Python programming language. Unlike some of the free options available, it has a front in with a visual component which makes additional types of visualization much easier as it does with program and data analysis. It also doubles as a Python library for those who are in to that sort of thing. This program was created by the University of Ljubljana and their Bioinformatics Laboratory of the Faculty of Computer and Information Sciences.

The individual components available in Orange Software are individually referred to as widgets and can be used for practically everything from basic data visualization to selecting subsets to empirical evaluation, preprocessing, predictive modeling, algorithm generation and more. Furthermore, visual programming can be successfully implemented through an interface which allows users to directly create workflows quickly and easily by linking together a predefined group of widgets. This doesn't stymie advanced users, however, as they are still free to alter widgets and manipulate data via Python.

The latest version of Orange Software includes many core components that were created in C++ with wrappers that were then created using Python. The installation defaults for the software include widget sets for supervised and unsupervised data analysis, regression, classification, visualization and data collection as well as other various algorithms and preprocessing tools. Orange Software is available online, for free, at Orange.biolab.si.

*R:* The programing language known simply as R is a great environment for software related to statistical computing as well as visualization options. It was created by the R Foundation for Statistical Computing and is commonly used by data miners and statisticians who are working on the creation of statistical programs or data analysis. R and the libraries that it is related to are useful when it comes to using numerous techniques, be they graphical or statistical. These include things like nonlinear modeling, linear modeling, time series analysis, clustering, classification and various statically tests.

Additional strengths include things like its ability to generate static graphics which means it can create interactive graphics and graphs that are publishing quality without any extra tweaking required. The fact that it is written in R also makes it easy for the novice analyst to look under the hood and determine how certain crucial decisions are being made which can lead to personal insight and growth as well as reliable predictive analytic results every time.

R was created in GNU which brings with it the usual caveats. Additionally, the source code for R is written in a mixture of R, Fortran and C. A binary version of the program is available for numerous operating systems and while the primary version does not support a graphical front end, there are numerous options for such things available online as well. It is available online at R-Project.org.

*Scikit-Learn:* Scikit-Learn is another type of software-based machine library written in Python. It also features different types of clustering, regression and classification algorithms including several that are less common in the open source space. Algorithms include DBSCAN, k-means, gradient boosting, random forests and support vector machines. It also works seamlessly with the SciPy and NumPy Python libraries which cover scientific libraries and numerical libraries respectively.

Scikit-Learn was created by David Cournapeau as part of the Google Summer of Code, though the code base was later rewritten by other developers. While it was not actively being iterated upon for several years, starting in 2015 it is once again under active development which makes it a great choice for those who don't care for the other options in the open source space that are in this list. Scikit-Learn can be found online, for free at Scikit-Learn.org.

*WEKA:* The Waikato Environment for Knowledge Analysis, WEKA, for short is a software suite that was written in Java by the University of Waikato in New Zealand. Unlike many open source analysis platforms, WEKA has multiple user interfaces that provide access to a wide variety of options. The preprocess panel allows users to import data from databases and filtering data through the use of preset algorithms. It also makes it possible to delete attributes or instances based on predefined criteria.

Additionally, the classify panel makes it easy for users to use either regression or classification algorithms based on different data sets and also determine the accuracy of the models that are created through the process. The associate panel is useful for users who are interested in gaining access to various algorithms that are useful when it comes to determining the various relationships that certain data points have with one another. The cluster panel is useful for those looking for more options when it comes to optimizing clustering effectively and includes the k-means algorithm as well as the maximization algorithm if you are interested in finding the normal distributions mixture.

Finally, the select attributes panel will allow users to access even more algorithms; this time they will be related to various predictive attributes that might be found in a given dataset. The visualize panel is useful for those who are interested in generating scatter plot matrixes which make it easy for scatter plots to be analyzed further based on the information they provide.

Dear Reader,

Connection Books Club wants to thank you for the purchase of one of our many informative eBooks! We hope you enjoyed your purchase and we want to invite you to join our club.

When you subscribe to our FREE club, you'll receive regular newsletters and incredible discounts on our bestselling books! Connection Books Club makes reading easy, giving you the content you want, at a price you can't believe. All that it takes to enroll in our FREE book club is your email. We'll send you the latest business and personal development news and highlight the newest books that are ready for you to enjoy.

> http://www.connectionbooksclub.com/bonus/

As part of your subscription, we're giving you a FREE download of one of our favorite eBooks, *Money Management: Learn How to Organize Your Financial Life and Invest in Your Future*. This eBook covers many financial situations, such as lowering interest rates and exploring options surrounding bankruptcy, helping you determine the best financial action for you.

Money management may be difficult for some people, but with your FREE copy of *Money Management: Learn How to Organize Your Financial Life and Invest in Your Future*, you'll learn the skills and information you need to make the best decisions to secure your financial future. The strategies contained in this eBook, designed for the everyday person, offering easy to follow steps and money saving tips.

Understanding money and how to make it works for you is important and with this eBook, you'll learn what you need to know to start building your financial security. Here are the top 5 reasons for reading *Money Management: Learn How to Organize Your Financial Life and Invest in Your Future*:

1. The strategies in this book are designed to help real people achieve their financial goals.
2. Explore different options for retirement.
3. Discover hacks for navigating the grocery store's subtle spending traps.
4. Inform yourself about how you might be able to get away with paying less than you owe on credit cards and other outstanding debts.
5. Experience a feeling of newfound freedom when you understand that you have every ability to live a life of financial stability.

➢ Get your copy here:
   http://www.connectionbooksclub.com/bonus/

The benefits of receiving this eBook for FREE are endless! Take control of your finances and start living the life you want.

By subscribing to Connection Books Club, not only will you get incredible discounts, our FREE welcome gift eBook, and a regular newsletter, but you'll also get the opportunity to receive FREE eBooks! Subscribers are invited to share reviews of the eBooks they've read, earning new titles at no cost! All it takes to enroll is your email. http://www.connectionbooksclub.com/bonus/

Discounts and free eBooks are just a click away! Enter your

email for VIP access to new books, incredible deals and money saving options, and even free giveaways! And don't forget, by signing up today for Connection Books Club, you'll receive the incredible eBook *Money Management: Learn How to Organize Your Financial Life and Invest in Your Future* for FREE!

Connection Books Club is excited to have you join our ranks of subscribers. We hope you enjoy your FREE eBook and all the great reading coming your way soon!

http://www.connectionbooksclub.com/bonus/

# Conclusion Wrap up: Data Analysis Overview

Thank for making it through to the end of *Data Analytics: An Introduction and Explanation into Predictive Analysis (How to Integrate Analytics into Your Business)*. Let's hope it was informative and able to provide you with all of the tools you need to achieve your goals both in the near term and for the months and years ahead. Remember, just because you've finished this book doesn't mean there is nothing left to learn on the topic. Becoming an expert at something is a marathon, not a sprint – slow and steady wins the race.

The next step is to stop reading already and to get ready to start using data analytics in general, and predictive analytics specifically, in all the ways that can directly benefit your business. Remember, while the steps to becoming a successful data analyst may seem complicated, if you keep at it, there is nothing you can't accomplish.

If you have enjoyed this book, I'd greatly appreciate if you could leave an honest review on Amazon.

Reviews are very important to us authors, and it only takes a minute to post.

Thank you

www.ingramcontent.com/pod-product-compliance
Lightning Source LLC
Chambersburg PA
CBHW061158180526
45170CB00002B/851